A BUSHIE'S
GUIDE TO LIFE

by Digger Cobb

Illustrations by Pete

BROLGA
PUBLISHING PTY. LTD.
· A.C.N. 063 962 443 ·

Published by Brolga Publishing Pty Ltd
ACN 063 962 443
P.O. Box 959, Ringwood,
Victoria 3134, Australia.

National Library of Australia
Cataloguing-in-Publication entry

ISBN 0-909608-06-7

Printed by Griffin Paperbacks, Adelaide.
Design and Production by Pro Art Design, Adelaide.

So you'll never be bushed...
Look up at the sky often -
but keep your feet on the ground.
Be as game as Ned Kelly - but don't be a dill.
Do the right things by your mates and
always make sure the beer is cold.

Digger Cobber Mate

A bushie never has more baggage
than he can carry.

If you don't stir the possum
it won't bite you.

Under the afternoon sun
even a bush rat has a big shadow.

Some tracks look smooth and easy to follow,
others are wider and harder to see -
but a good pair of boots will
get you through both.

If you've hit the bastard and he still won't go down - buy him a beer instead.

Remember,
even a kick up the bum is a step forward.

Townies are a few 'roos short
in the top paddock.

Good bush tucker feeds our body
but a good bush yarn feeds our dreams.

Never criticise another bushie unless you've spent a day carrying his swag.

YOU SHOULD USE A SUITCASE. THEY'RE MUCH MORE CONVENIENT

Two up is like being in love.
No one wins nothing unless the coins match.

If you always watch where you're walking
you'll miss the dog shit -
but you'll miss the sunset too.

A townie can search for years
for what the bushie has at his campfire.

When Lady Luck comes your way
lend a hand to the bloke on the floor -
you never know when you'll be there.

Bullshit
Baffles
Brains.

A nervous man is like a nervous horse -
wild-eyed and sweaty -
and you can't trust either.

If you think you're gunna do it
and say you're gunna do it -
bloody well do it.

Before you ask a mate for a loan
decide which one you need the most.

Everyone should own an Akubra hat.

Don't mess with something that isn't messing with you.

The boss can give you the shits
but the cook can give you the runs.

The smallest dog can still piss
on the biggest tree.

Tickle the till and
you won't be laughing for long.

Some people (and books) are as useless as tits on a bull.

If you always put on a dingo act
people will treat you like a dog.

Some fellas are so tight they can get three feeds out of a pink galah AND make soup from the bones!

No one likes a dobber.

If you charge through the nose,
expect to be paid in snot.

You may crave a cuppa
but the billy will never boil
if you don't light the fire.

If you run around like a headless chook
you're bound to fall down dead
sooner or later.

When you're between waterholes
if you dawdle, you're dead -
unless there's a pub in the middle.

A Bushman's Curse:
May your chickens turn into emus
and kick your dunny down.

You can be surrounded by people
and still feel as lonely as a country dunny.

A drongo is a mate who has forgotten it's his turn to shout.

You'll always find water
if you keep digging where you started.

You may think you're a hot shot
but try getting someone else's
cattle dog to obey you.

Let your temper be like a bush track -
the dust flies high but settles quickly.

When you're in a fight and you've got two hands tied behind your back remember the advice your ol' man gave you - use your head.

If your heart is in the right place -
so is your head.

A word of warning:
Don't talk with your mouth full or people
might notice that it's full of bull.

The only way to end a blue
is to shout the other bloke a drink.

You can "stone the bloody crows"
but if you do be prepared for it to rain rocks.

Those who expect to be hunted will be.

A comfy homestead is fine but give a bushie a sniff of a muster and he'll be saddled up and out there before you know it.

True mates are like dogs,
some are pedigrees, some are mongrels
but treat them right and they'll always
come when you need them.

Watch what you click if you're shearing in the nick.

A true bushie never flinches
from the midday sun -
just deepens the squint.

You may be selling tickets on yourself but watch that you're not the only one buying.

No one gets a tin arse by sitting on it.

To save your skin
all you need is a quick fist and a fast horse ...

... But to save your soul
watch a sunset on a clear night.

If you drink alone
it will always be your shout.

Keep a grin on your mug
when things are down
and you'll always have
true mates around.

Some people are like flies -
they don't care if they hang around
cow shit or lamingtons.

Put your strides on before your boots
or you could land on your face.

You can put on a clean shirt and shine your boots everyday but if you only bathe once a week you'll still attract blowies.

Everyone makes a galah of themself at sometime
but if you make a habit of it
people will think you're a bit of a cockatoo.

Never judge a man
by the size of his brim.

The best things in life are free -
which is beaut when you're stoney broke.

An emu is a hell'va big bird
but it doesn't get off the ground.

Talk slow but let your brain think fast.

It's not the leaving that makes you cry,
just the dust in your eyes.

Trust in God -
but always tie up your horse.

If you want to win the race
put your head down
and dig your heels in.

Let sleeping dogs lie -
unless they're lying in your bed.

A billy takes time to boil
but the time spent waiting
can sweeten the tea.

The bigger the fire
the bigger the fool.

If you're not happy with the way
you make a quid it will never bring you
anything of value.

Never make a promise you can't keep.

It only takes a dry twig to
start a raging bushfire.

An occasional flutter on the horses
keeps a man honest and humble.

Everyone can follow a different track
but they all end up looking
at the same sunset.

A good woman will wait till the cows come home but if they're full of bull when they arrive - she won't be around for the next milking.

People are like beer -
some are better than others.

Even the head cocky
makes a galah of himself sometimes.

If you play possum too often
you could end up a dead one.

Let your worries go like pissin' in the dust on a hot day.

Beach flies stick like shit
to a wet blanket.

If you roll your own you'll always know
what you're smoking.

Beware:
Spin too big a yarn
and you'll end up in knots.

Never miss a good chance
to shut your trap.

A dark horse can be a fair cow -
especially if you didn't back it.

If you've got shit for brains
what comes out your bum?

It looks easy to swim across
a slow moving river
but watch for dangerous snags.

Real mates stick by you through thick and thin
but the parasites soon drop off
under the heat of the midday sun.

Whingers usually find themself
with a lot of space around them.

The bush can be paradise one minute -
next it's trying to kill you.
That's the challenge and that's why we love it.

Never tell a yarn on a dry throat.

If you carry on like a pork chop
chances are you'll end up
covered in gravy.

There'll be plenty of time to rest
when you're six foot under.

You've got something to say, say it.
Say it straight and say it clear -
and make sure nothings in the way
of you and the back door.

The trouble with going fishing is that there's always some silly bastard who wants to fish!

New billies don't make good tea.

A bushie never pokes around in hollow logs because not all surprises are good ones.

An Akubra can be more comfortable
than a good homestead.

Humour is always welcome around the campfire.

A true mate knows when it's his turn
to swing the billy.

Never trust a man who doesn't meet your eye.

Live life like a wombat -
eats roots, shoots, and leaves.

When you go outside always make sure
the flywire screen door is open
or you could strain yourself.

Feed and water your horse first
and you'll always have a quick getaway.

It only takes one mozzie buzzing in your ear to ruin a good nights sleep.

If you've got a beef
take it to the head cow.

Treat a woman like a high spirited horse -
never take either for granted.

Wet your whistle too often
and you'll end up blowing raspberries.

Some people are like a callous -
they always show up when the work is over.

Rain on wheat can be like a woman's love
too much ruins it
but not enough dries it out.

Make sure the bastards dead before you skin it.

Red sky at sunset means a fair dawning
but a red sky at dawn is a
bushman's warning.

Some politicians couldn't run a chook raffle in a country pub.

Blow-ins are never invited and worse -
they never shout a beer.

Don't fight the land.
Accept the droughts and floods and the clear
blue skies and live through them all.

Be the first to say G'day, Ooroo or Coo-ee
and you're sure to be remembered.

If you're up shit creek in a barbed wire canoe without a paddle - you're stuffed.

Good tucker is always tastier shared.

Never cut a tree when
just the branch will do.

Don't be like green wood,
all smoke and no fire.

You can fight a fire from the front or from behind but when there's fire all around put your head between your knees and kiss your arse goodbye.

We can try all our life to own the land
but when we're dead and six feet under
who owns who then?

If you chew on a problem long enough
you'll end up spitting chips.

Before you decide to lay down and die
find yourself a comfortable spot.

A sky full of stars,
a waterhole, and a tree.
Life doesn't get any better than this.

Keep a swag on your shoulder
and you'll always be close to home.

Ta...to all these mates:
Jim the Jackeroo,
Paul from the West - a real galah,
Big Stiff for keeping the billy boiling,
Deb who drinks like a lizard at midday,
Whitey for always checking the dunny seat.
Ooroo I'm off like a bucket of prawns in the
midday sun - D.C.M.

Psst, if you want to have a bash at being a Bushie,
send us your saying,
c/o P.O. Box 959,
Ringwood, Victoria 3134, Australia.